THE GRANDFATHER

My Grandad is the Best Chef in the World

By

PAUL JAMES

Shield Crest

ISBN: 978-1-913839-36-9

MMXXI

A CIP catalogue record for this
is available from the British Library

Published by
ShieldCrest Publishing,
Bicker, Lincs, PE20 3BT England
Tel: +44 (0) 333 8000 890
www.shieldcrest.co.uk

DEDICATION

My Three beautiful grandchildren, Freya, Freddy and Summer-Rai, who not only helped with the cooking and listened intently to my stories of the past but destroyed my Kitchen with flour, eggs, a sink full of washing up and a constant use of my vacuum.

But I wouldn't change them for anything, they, along with my own children, family and friends brighten my world.

Yes, sometimes I wish I could change my name from "Grandad can I have" or "Grandad can you just play with my dolls or toy soldiers" ......but no not really, in fact never, because this book is more about love than cooking.... cooking just brings you closer, enjoying the bonding and creativity that it brings.

I really hope that this book brings you the joy and happiness that it brought to me.

MAKING MEMORIES THAT WILL BE PASSED ON FROM GENERATION TO GENERATION.

I also want to thank ShieldCrest Publishing for making this publication possible

Foreword By : CYRUS TODIWALA

This book is written with passion and love not just from a grandfather's eyes, but from the excited eyes of those young souls that have been blessed forever by the magic of creating great dishes from simple everyday ingredients that adults take for granted.

This is a fantastic book for me and for the whole community of chefs at large, teaching from a very early stage in life will enable a love of cooking that will serve our youngsters through the generations of time.

Imagine at one time our youngest child used to tell everyone that: "My dad is the best cook in the world "but for a young grandchild saying "my grandad is the best chef in the world" that is amazing and just these few words mean that: "Grandad you may be the best now, but we are coming very close and will one day become great chefs too".

I wish my good friend Paul all the success he deserves with his book, and I hope that it will inspire other parents and grandparents to view everything they do with food as an education to themselves and their children.

As The Indian art of Ayurveda says: 'No harm could ever come out of cooking great food simply'. And that which the Great Hippocrates put into words quite simply in

323BC: "Let Food be Thy Medicine and Medicine Be Thy Food".

Enjoy
Cyrus Todiwala OBE DL DBA

Good friend and world-renowned Chef.

INTRODUCTION.

Having to retire as a professional chef because of a serious illness at the early age of 45 in 2017, I decided to create my own food and travel blog called 'Recipes From My Travels', helping businesses in the hospitality and tourism industry plus writing and creating recipes from my visits locally and from around the world.

Now it's 2021, I'm still grateful for life and I'm so lucky to have a loving family and great friends by my side.

Since 2018, when I created my blog, I have been lucky enough to have added to the beautiful places that I've visited, here in the UK and around the world......even more so to write about my experiences.

In the space of a couple of years I've became a published author with my first book "Recipes from My Travels, Great Britain and Cornwall edition one".

I've had two eBooks: "New York, New York" which is my own personal and emotional diary of my youngest Son, Jay's and my visit to New York and another cookbook called "Recipes from My Kitchen".

Along With my children I have created two other food blogs, 'Completely Cornwall' and 'Brummagem Rubs & Spices'.

We have our own website under the logo "RFMT" where we continue to promote businesses in the hospitality and tourism industry around the world. On the website it has an online shop where you can purchase our own cookbooks, merchandise and our very own brand of rubs and spices and seasoned sea salts, all made by the "RFMT" family.

I've also been fortunate to have been asked by local newspapers *"Bromsgrove Standard"* and the *"Coventry observer"* and *"Voyagers Voice"* magazine to write food and travel articles and regular feature columns.

And with over 8,000 followers and millions of reaches worldwide, we continue to grow.

✱✱✱✱✱✱✱✱✱✱✱✱✱

The idea behind the book came from one of my three grandchildren, Freya who kept on telling her teachers at school and probably anyone else that would listen, that she always helped her grandad cook, because; "He is a chef" and; "my Grandad is the best chef in the world", something that I won't discourage her from saying until she's old enough to realise I'm not.

It took me back to when I was younger helping my lovely neighbour Auntie Winnie, who would look after me while my mother and father were at work and do lunch. When I say 'help', it was usually mashing the potatoes.....incidentally I still use the very same potato masher from *Auntie Winnie,* it must be close on 50 years old.

As a retired chef I personally believe that children should be encouraged with the help of an adult, from an early age to know the basics of cooking....after all it's an important part of life, just as paying your bills and going out to work.

Here I have put together, with the help of my three sous chefs and beautiful grandchildren Freya, Freddy and Summer-Rai, easy to follow, adult friendly dishes, to cook together.

The dishes are in no particular order....it's for kids to enjoy, no starter, desserts or main courses here.....just children enjoying to learn how to cook.

All the best and enjoy Freya, Freddy, and Summer-Rai. Oh yeah and me, chief washer-upper.

MESSAGES OF SUPPORT

I haven't known Paul long. From what we have talked about, I know he is a person of heart ! His grandchildren, food and the way he writes has to be the best combination ever! Just like amazing food that has the best ingredients!
Jennifer Arnold
Good friend and cook

I've known Paul James now for some time, he is a gentleman, charismatic and affectionate 'Brummie' whom I'm proud and humbled to call a friend.

"The Grandfather, my Grandad is the best Chéf in the World", epitomises Paul as a brilliant cook, who's inspiration oozes from his long travels to the beautiful islands of Greece, and our own spectacular Cornish Coasts. Enjoy!!
Matt Davies
Good friend and Vice President of the British Culinary Federation

Paul James' new book The Grandfather is a wonderful collection of easy and delicious recipes which will bring joy to children and adults alike as they cook together and then share their achievements as they eat their creations.

Cooking is a basic and important life skill which can give you a great deal of personal satisfaction, help you to learn how to nourish your body so it functions healthily but most of all it's so much fun...and it could even become your career or help you inspire others to cook too.

So why not grab a copy of 'The Grandfather', pop on an apron, gather the family together and have a go?

Happy cooking.
Sonia Duthie
Good friend and 2019 Masterchef Uk Quarter Finalist.

Paul James, The true "The Grandfather" is a kind , brave, down to earth gentleman, who, despite serious illnesses, is proving to be an inspiration for many, both inside and outside of the world of hospitality.
Nadine Saunders Drover
Good Friend.

If you are looking for inspiration across the smorgasbord of life, you need to look no further than chef extraordinaire and great friend of mine, Paul James.

Paul's passion, ambition and drive is evident in every encounter with him. I admire this great man's tenacity, his big heart and love for his family is truly remarkable.

Seeing Paul with his grandchildren is heart melting.
I have been lucky enough to have Paul collaborate with me on my book, his recipes are, indeed, the personification of looking good enough to eat!

I'm honoured to be this, chef and a gentleman's, good friend.

Paul has so many talents and great ideas, I am certain, that along with his enthusiasm, zest for life and heartfelt

compassion, Paul will be a massive success with a Midas touch.
Fiona Lou Collins
Good Friend and Author of 'Dirty Dishes - Recipes to ignite passion'.

I wish Paul the very best with his book. We spoke recently about his upcoming book, and he deserves all the very best.
Nesta Wyn Ellis
Good Friend, Novelist, Biographer, Screenwriter and personal biographer of former PM John Major.

As a teacher and a Mum of two young boys, this cookbook with easy to follow steps, fresh and accessible ingredients is the perfect combination of fun and deliciousness.
Samantha Geerlings Bowen
Teacher

Good luck Paul with the book and we are looking forward to collaborating with you in the future, great things happen when great people work together.
Michelle & Lilith Holsey-Sheppard, Good friends and owners at Butchers Block Bromsgrove, Worcestershire.

I met Paul at catering college, and we worked as a team throughout the entire course.
Paul James is not only a talented chef, but a loyal and supportive colleague. I'm really proud of what he has achieved, and I can't wait to read his new book. I'm also looking forward to working with him again in the future."
Rachael Wright
Good friend and Chef

Paul James is the kindest person and an amazing friend, he is a true fighter and deserves only the best, I wish Paul all the luck in the world with his new book and I know that it's going to be a huge success.
Paulina Bennett
Good Friend

Summer enjoyed every second helping her Grandad in the kitchen, what she was taught there, she brought home here and wanted to continue to learn.
Daniella Mckeever
Paul's Daughter and mother of Summer-Rai

Freya and Freddy always love visiting their Grandad, especially as they know they maybe helping out in the kitchen with their Grandad to cook their meals.
Mark James
Paul's Son and father of Freya and Freddy

Watching my nephew and nieces learn about cooking techniques and of course my dad's funny and humorous stories and ways of explaining the recipes and how they evolved were lovely to watch, but if they decide to write another edition, I'm keeping out of the way with the mess left in the kitchen after these three were let loose…Haha.
Jay James
Paul's Son and uncle of Freya, Freddy and Summer-Rai

Contents

INTRODUCTION. 6

SHORTBREAD COOKIES 1

HOMEMADE CHEESE & ONION SAUSAGE ROLLS 3

CURRIED COTTAGE PIE 6

PEPPERONI PIZZA 9

PASTA with VEGETABLE PASTA SAUCE 12

POSH GROWN UP FISH FINGER SANDWICHES 14

KIDS KEEMA FRIED RICE & AND A BRUMMIE EGG & POTATO CURRY 16

MINI ROAST BEEF DINNER WITH BUTTERED VEGETABLES 20

DECONSTRUCTED APPLE CRUMBLE 25

NOT SO LEMONY SORBET 27

AUNTIE WINNIE'S SAUSAGE & MASH 30

TOAD IN THE HOLE 32

HOMEMADE CHOCOLATE & STRAWBERRY CORNFLAKE FLURRY 34

CHINESE CHOPPED CHICKEN CURRY WITH RICE 36

MARINATED GINGER & LIME MELON KEBABS 40

KIDS POSH HAM & CHEESE TOASTIE OR CROQUE MADAME . 42

CORNISH SPLITS... 45

GREAT NANS BEST STEW EVER 48

MINCE BEEF PIE... 55

SHORTBREAD COOKIES

As a young lad growing up and maybe only up until recently I disliked cooking desserts or sweets of any kind, it just never really interested me....maybe it was because I was never a sweet kind of person, more savoury.

It's a pity I never showed more interest, I think cake making is an art itself along with producing amazing desserts, saying that if I had shown more attention and desire I would have probably been knee deep in black forest gateau, tiramisu or beignets with the Grandchildren instead of cookie dough mix and fighting to stop them eating it before it left the bowl.

This is definitely a recipe to get the kids involved with, it's ideal for showing them how to measure out all the ingredients in little dishes ready to be weighed on their own mini scales.

The choice of cutters you use is up to the kids, so they chose a car and unicorn, unfortunately life size Princess castles and Tyrannosaurus Rex shape cutters were unavailable in the local supermarket.

Ingredients

Unsalted salted butter, room temperature
granulated sugar

1 teaspoon vanilla extract
Plain flour

Method

In the bowl mix the butter, sugar and vanilla together. Slowly add the flour and combine.

Preheat oven to 180c Line a baking sheet with parchment paper and set aside.

Roll dough out into a large square, 1/3-inch thick. Cut the dough into any shape you want using cookie cutters.

Place on baking sheet and bake for 18-20 minutes.

Transfer to a wire rack to cool

HOMEMADE CHEESE & ONION SAUSAGE ROLLS

Sausage rolls always remind me of Christmas time. It's part of tradition watching these little bites of loveliness go into the oven and come out all golden and flaky.

Which takes me back to a story when I was little and popping round with my mom to "Auntie Winnies" who lived next door, she and her husband "Uncle Alf" were an elderly couple who used to look after me while my mom and dad was at work.

Anyway on this one visit at Christmas time, the beautiful aroma of cooked sausage rolls filled the air as I burst through the front door, seeing these delicately and precision like placed sausage rolls cooling on a rack, I was quickly told not to touch them as they were "baking hot" after just coming out the oven...well I'm sorry to say I disappeared upstairs to "go to the loo" with 4 sausage rolls burning through my trouser pockets and onto my skin, I wasn't bothered, they tasted delicious....over the years as I got older I felt guilty about "Borrowing" these four sausage rolls, not because I had taken them, even though it was wrong.....but guilty for "Uncle Alf" as he got the blame for eating them !!

Ingredients

Ready to roll puff pastry
Sausage meat
Spring onions
Grated Cheese
Salt & pepper
1 Beaten egg

Method

Remove the pastry from the refrigerator and Let it come to room temperature.
Heat the oven to 180c.

Slice the spring onions thinly and place to one side in a bowl.

When the pastry has come to room temperature and manageable, roll out onto a clean floured surface.

In a bowl add the sausage meat, spring onions and grated cheese. Lightly season with salt & pepper and gently mix it all together.

just off centre to the pastry, roll out to an even sausage shape.

Brush the edges with the beaten egg and carefully fold the pastry over and gently seal down the edges.

Brush the sausage roll with the beaten egg mixture and cut into roughly 2 inch size pieces.

Place on a greaseproof lined baking tray with plenty of space in between the sausage rolls and cook for about twenty minutes until golden brown and cooked thoroughly right through.

Always use a meat thermometer if unsure.

Remove from the oven and leave to cool down before eating.

CURRIED COTTAGE PIE

Today in the amazingly cultural society we live in, our youngsters are lucky to experience the different tastes and flavours from around the world.

Spices such as chillies, coriander, turmeric and cumin etc...and herbs of the Mediterranean such as oregano. To our little ones these flavours are a thing of normality, herbs in lasagne or cumin in curries...in my day it was spaghetti hoops on toast and the hottest curried beans my brother Allan could make...This dish combines two cultural and culinary traditions...Curried cottage pie.

I Always let the children mash the potatoes, because that would be the first thing they see as it comes out of the oven, this will give them great joy and pride knowing that the mash was theirs and it was the best mash in the whole world and all the hard work you put in with the heat of the mince cooking and eyes watering because of the onion chopping, didn't really matter as the look on the children's face said it all.......Priceless.

I should know I was that young boy once with a potato masher....

Ingredients

500 grams of lean steak mince.
2 carrots, thinly
1 onion, thinly sliced
200 grams of cooked garden Peas.
4 large Maris piper potatoes.
1 stock cube.
2 tablespoons of mild curry powder.
Generous knob of Butter for the mashed potato topping.
100 ml of whole milk for the mashed potato topping.

Method

Peel the potatoes and cut into chunks. Place in a saucepan of lightly salted COLD water, bring to the boil then cover and simmer until cooked.

In a frying pan brown the steak mince, drain excess oil and put in a bowl and leave to one side for the moment.

Clean out the pan and fry the onions and carrots, until the onions are soft.

Add the mince back into the pan and crumble in the Stock cube and curry powder, mix well then add a drop of boiling water.
Combine well.

Put the mince mixture into a ovenproof dish and pipe on the mashed potato.
Cook in a preheated oven 180c for about 25-35 minutes or until the mashed potato topping is golden and the mince is piping hot and cooked thoroughly.

Serve with fries and a bowl of buttered garden peas.

PEPPERONI PIZZA

What kids can't resist a pizza, any mismatch of toppings you like, drenched in a sauce base and smothered in gooey melted cheese. Well that was probably my first mistake, giving them a choice, realising that I would be force fed the concoction of culinary delights that they came up with for me to try...without exception !! I had to come up quickly with a bit of negotiating that comes as you all know only to well with parenting and child minding.

We eventually came up with mixed peppers, pepperoni slices and loads of mozzarella cheese covering finely sliced vinegar flavoured cucumber....Gerkhins didn't sound as appealing to my three, but what they didn't know, didn't hurt them to try.

They enjoyed it immensely, more than I would have if it had been broccoli, oranges, chocolate, strawberries and fizzy cola bottles they wanted to use........plus I didn't have to threaten them with locking them in the cupboard with the bogeyman if they didn't change their minds........Only joking !!

Ingredients

Medium size pizza base
100 grams of barbecue sauce
Pepperoni Slices
Handful of mozzarella cheese
Gerkhins diced finely
Mix peppers diced finely

Method

Spread the pizza base with the barbecue sauce.

Arrange the pepperoni around the base along with the gerkhins and peppers.

Scatter a good quantity of grated mozzarella cheese over the pizza and bake in a preheated oven at 180c until the cheese is bubbling.
Cool down and serve.

Sous chef Freddy

PASTA with VEGETABLE PASTA SAUCE

Such a simple dish for the kids to help with, plus by cutting the veggies up really small and adding a splash of pasta sauce to coat them with they are taking in all the goodness without to much persuasion.

Fortunately, my little ones don't mind vegetables, so using less pasta sauce and more vegetables was a bonus.

Cut up some baguettes and let them make the cheesy garlic bread this will keep them occupied while you do the adult part of the cooking.

Ingredients

100grams dried penne pasta (or any other pasta, if using fresh, change cooking times accordingly)

1 sliced courgette.
1 sliced red pepper.
Splash of pasta sauce to coat.
Cheesy Garlic bread to serve.

Method

Bring a large pan of salted water to the boil.

While that's waiting to boil, in a heated frying pan add a drop of oil and gently fry the vegetables until soft.

Add the pasta to the boiling water and cook as package instructions tell you.

Drain the pasta and add to the soft vegetables, add the pasta sauce and gently heat through.

Serve with the cheesy garlic bread.

POSH GROWN-UP FISH FINGER SANDWICHES

Fish finger sandwiches.....proper comfort food and theirs nothing wrong with good quality supermarket fish fingers, but it's nice for the little ones to actually see what goes into them.

Plus it's a lot less complicating than trying to explain why I had chopped of the "little fishes fingers" and that fish don't have fingers and........well you get what I mean.

Served with a plain bag of crisps and the little blue bag of salt to tip over them...perfect.

Ingredients

1 small fillet of skinless and boneless cod
Batter mix

1 beaten egg
100grams of flour
2 slices of bread
Shredded Iceberg lettuce
Sliced cherry tomatoes
Sliced cucumber
Caper Mayonnaise (optional)
Packet of crisps.
Enough vegetable oil to cook

Method

Cut the cod fillet into Goujons (always check for small bones, even if you buy boneless)

In three separate bowls add the made-up batter mix, flour and one beaten egg.

With each goujon dip into the egg, flour and batter mix and carefully place into the hot oil and cook until cooked thoroughly through.

Drain on some kitchen paper.

Prepare your sandwich by spreading caper mayonnaise (or butter) on one side of the bread.

Then add your shredded lettuce, tomatoes and cucumber.

Add the cod Goujons on top and serve with some crisps.

KIDS KEEMA FRIED RICE & AND A BRUMMIE EGG & POTATO CURRY

This dish sums up memories of when I was a little lad growing up in a multi cultural and vibrant city.

Which is something that I like to teach my Grandchildren, not only are we are all equal but to enjoy and explore the different flavours and tastes from the food brought to us from other parts of the world.

Visiting different areas of the city threw up various and distinguished smells and flavours, none more so than the aromas of curries being made.

Unfortunately growing up in the 70s and 80s it was very rare that we had an Indian meal.

In fact I remember with affection my mum only ever cooking a packet 'vesta' curry and always with grated cheese on top and popped under a hot grill until the cheese started bubbling. A couple of 'rounds of bread and butter' and I was happy.

In fact, I'm not going to lie, if I ever see a 'vesta curry' in the shop, which is getting rarer, I always more often than not buy it.

But sadly, to be honest, it's not the same as my lovely childhood memories of my mum standing at the stove and plating up my curry, placed with the sauce in a circle of the glistening white boiled rice.

So, this recipe is homage to my hometown city of Birmingham and memories of the Rag Market, Rotunda and of course the Bull in the Bullring shopping centre.

Ingredients

Handful of boiled new potatoes
3 free range eggs softly boiled
1 red onion sliced
1 tsp of chilli powder
1 tsp of turmeric powder (half in the curry & Half in the rice)
1 tsp of cumin powder
Selection of Finely chopped green and red chillies
400 ml coconut milk
Cooked basmati rice
100 grams good quality lamb mince
1/2 tsp Garam Masala
1/2 tsp of curry powder
Coriander leaves for garnish

Method

1. Gently fry the chilli powder, half the turmeric powder, cumin powder, in a little drop of oil to take out the slight rawness of the powder, add a splash of water.
2. Then add your onions and chopped chillies.
3. Fry until soft.
4. Next add your coconut milk and bring to the boil stirring continuously, add the boiled potatoes and reduce heat and let it simmer.
5. Next brown your lamb mince and discard any oil, add the rest of your turmeric powder, curry powder and Garam Masala and gently cook for a few minutes.
6. Then add the cooked rice and stir making sure every grain is coated in the delicate mince mixture.
7. Cook until the lamb is completely cooked.
8. Finally add your eggs to the curry and serve with a scatter of chopped coriander.

Sous chef Summer-Rai

MINI ROAST BEEF DINNER WITH BUTTERED VEGETABLES

This is something really from my childhood. Plus I've left the Grandchildren to wash up....

So as I love a bit of nostalgia and as a 70's kid brought up in West Heath, Birmingham I thought I would share this little story.

I really do hope you can relate to some of it........and not look at me as some member of a chicken neck eating crazy family.

Sunday dinners or roasts when I was a young lad was a memorable time. I remember playing football outside and smelling the waft in the air of a Sunday dinner being cooked from different households in our road.

Roast chicken mainly as it was the cheaper option in the 70's, not that I was aware of that anyway.

I remember with fondness the cabbage being cooked for about 5 hours, along with the vegetables! Pinching a roast potato or a stuffing ball to spread on a slice of bread while mom wasn't looking!! My brother Allan and my two sisters, Diane and Lorraine along with myself was always arguing who was going to eat the chicken liver or skin...........Or the neck!!!

I could just imagine my grandchildren fighting over the little bag of treats that were stuck up a chickens Bum......Somehow I don't think so.

My Dad and my Uncle Brian always went to the local pub on a Sunday dinnertime, waiting patiently outside with the usual regulars 10 minutes before opening time at 12 o'clock Playing darts for 50p a game, arguing whose round it was and occasionally hearing stories of the "regulars" dropping their false teeth in their pints, so nobody drank it while they went to the toilet!! Only then to find when returning that there were two sets of false teeth in the glass and everyone rolling about laughing......And all this in the space of two hours before the pub closed its doors until the evening!!!

My Dad always brought bags of crisps back afterwards for us kids, then I'd watch as my elder siblings argued what flavours they should have.

My Dad was always happy, cheerful and funny but this multiplied tenfold after a couple of pints of bitter, sloppily swearing his love to my mom before she sent him off to bed for his Sunday afternoon Nap.

Memories like these will be cherished and never forgotten.

When I say things have changed, I mean it not in a bad way but the tradition has gone with the ever fast changing of today's society, people being to busy rushing around shopping or working and it's easier and more convenient to order take-aways now.

Our roast dinner what my little sous chefs help cook was slightly different to then and I'm not sure my mom or the moms and dads of families up and down the country who stood tirelessly over the stove would believe cabbage could be cooked 4hrs and 45 minutes less than they did it or tinned carrots and peas that slowly simmered away for a couple of hours, turning slightly grey in colour as the water was topped up if required.

But these were memories of my childhood, and we were lucky to have good ones....

Is it my turn now to be old fashioned when i say that roasting a joint of beef for under an hour or blanching freshly prepared vegetables until al dente then gently sautéed in butter until they are glistening, especially now when today's younger generation are ordering pizzas and kebabs for Sunday lunch......

Just shows how quickly food and society evolves but it's one thing I always try and do when the grandchildren are staying and that's cook them a "proper Sunday dinner" I still believe some family traditions should carry on.

Ingredients

Small roasting joint of beef
New potatoes
2 sprouting broccoli
2 large carrot
200 grams sprouts
Salt and pepper
Olive oil
Fresh thyme
Fresh rosemary
1 Lemon halved
Butter
Yorkshire pudding
A few capers.

Method

Pre heat the oven to 180c.

To prepare the beef joint, season with salt and pepper and in a hot frying pan add a small knob of butter until foaming and seal in all sides to hold in the flavour. Then place in a ovenproof dish, add a drizzle of oil on top and Scatter over some fresh thyme and Rosemary.

Cover with foil and Cook in the oven.

Cook the beef for 30 mins if you like it rare, 40 mins for medium and 1 hr for well done.

Remove and let the joint rest for half hour before slicing.

Prepare and cook the broccoli, carrots (whole) and sprouts in boiling water until soft but still with a bit of firmness.

Drain, slice the carrots, and fry all the vegetables gently in a knob of butter until sweet and tender.

In another saucepan place your potatoes in cold water and bring to the boil, cover and simmer for 10 minutes. Drain and place in a baking tray with salt and pepper a squeeze of lemon and a tiny amount of oil. Cut 1 half of the lemon into wedges and place in between the potatoes and cook in the oven until crispy but soft in the middle.

Follow the recipe for Yorkshire Pudding on page 29 – 'Toad in the Hole'.

Serve with a scattering of capers and of course oxo gravy.

DECONSTRUCTED APPLE CRUMBLE

Another comfort food dessert made even simpler for the little ones, especially as they prepare most of the dish with obviously a little help from the elders.

Ingredients
4 peeled and Sliced apples (Pink lady)
1 teaspoon of powdered sweet Cinnamon for the apples
1 tablespoon of sweet cinnamon for the crumble
175g plain flour
110g golden caster sugar
110g cold butter
Pinch of salt.

Method

Heat the oven to 180c

In a small frying pan add the apples and cinnamon powder and gently caramelise until soft.

Put 175g plain flour and 110g golden caster sugar in a bowl with a good pinch of salt.
Add 110g cubed cold butter and rub it in with your fingertips until the mixture looks like breadcrumbs, add the remaining cinnamon powder.

Place the crumble mix onto a baking tray and put in a preheated oven for 25 minutes or until golden.

Arrange the apple slices onto a plate and sprinkle the crumble mix generously over the top.

Serve with lemon sorbet (see next recipe).

NOT SO LEMONY SORBET

Another little treat that was unheard of when I was younger!! We had ice cream...yes, fruit fresh from the tin...yes, custard powder...most definitely but lemons, with the peel being taken off and frozen with sugar and lemon squash, stirred occasionally before being put back into the freezer only to repeat half an hour later.....SURELY it's just posh slush puppies, or so the little ones said as it was taken out of the freezer for about the fifth time. Telling them at this stage that it was a mouth cleansing treat for after lunch didn't cut any ice with them as they searched in the kitchen draws for the curly straws to plunge into the frozen food container I was holding in my hand....

Puzzlement and amusement spread across their faces as I was trying to kernel the sorbet with a couple of spoons and place it gently onto a cut out piece of sponge cake.

They did enjoy it though and hopefully one day when they have children they will tell them of the time Grandad messed about with a slush puppy and two spoons.

Ingredients

250g white caster sugar
thick strip of lemon peel, thinly sliced
juice of 2 lemons
100grams of lemon cordial undiluted.

Method

Heat 250ml of water in a saucepan add the sugar and the lemon peel until the sugar has dissolved then bring the mixture to the boil. Cook for 3 mins then turn off the heat and leave to cool.

Pick out the lemon peel and discard.

Measure out 100ml of lemon cordial and lemon juice and add to the sugar mixture

Pour into a plastic container and freeze for 1hr 30 mins then mix up with a whisk to break up and incorporate the ice crystals which will be starting to form before returning to the freezer.

Keep mixing the sorbet once or twice every hour to break up the ice crystals. Stop mixing when firm but still manageable.

Serve the sorbet with a sponge cake, strawberries and a strawberry sauce and a light powdering of icing sugar.

Solus chef Freya

AUNTIE WINNIE'S SAUSAGE & MASH

This is one of my all time favourite comfort foods and I know my little ones love it.

The mash potato is silky and smooth and done with a bit of care it can beat any mash made with a potato ricer or sieve.

Slow cooked, good quality pork sausage is a must and served with old school Bisto gravy with oxo cubes and a couple of "rounds of bread to mop it up" is always a winner at Grandads.

The Grandfather

Ingredients

Good quality sausages
2 large potatoes peeled and cut into chunks
Butter
Milk
Salt and pepper

Method

In a heated frying pan, add a drop of oil and gently and slowly cook the sausage, never prick the sausage.

In a saucepan add the potatoes and fill with COLD water, bring to the boil, cover then simmer until cooked.

Drain the potatoes, add the milk, butter and salt and pepper and mash until no lumps.

Place the cooled down mash into a piping bag (optional) and arrange on a plate with the sausages, some vegetables of your choice and some oxo & Bisto onion gravy.

TOAD IN THE HOLE

Please whatever you do, don't call it toad in the hole in front of the little ones, convincing them it's nothing to do with green frog like creatures, that have big bulging eyes and jump around is something you do not want to go through but if you want to sit through a couple of hours of you tube videos showing what toad in the hole is, on your head be it.

Ingredients

140g plain flour
Good quality sausages
4 free range eggs
180 ml of milk
Vegetable oil

Method

Heat the oven to 200C

To make the batter, tip 140g plain flour into a bowl and beat in 4 eggs until smooth.

Gradually add 200ml milk and carry on beating until the mix is completely smooth.

Pour the batter into a plastic jug and place in the fridge, while you cook the sausages slowly without pricking them until cooked.

Add a tiny amount of oil to a Yorkshire pudding tray or small casserole dish and place in the oven for 5-6 minutes or until it gets hot.

Now this is where you have to get the sausages ready and the batter mix out of the fridge, because it's important to get your toad in the hole assembled and back into the oven as quickly as possible.

Take the dish out of the oven carefully, put one or two sausages in each one and add the batter mix half way up....you should be able to hear the mixture sizzle as you are pouring.

Place gently back into the oven for around twenty minutes UNTOUCHED until the batter has risen.

Remove from the oven and place on a paper towel to take away the excess cooing oil.

HOMEMADE CHOCOLATE & STRAWBERRY CORNFLAKE FLURRY

What more can I say to describe this recipe, just make sure the dust pan and brush is ready for all the smashed up chocolate cornflakes flying around like a broken up meteor falling from the sky.

Definitely an easy one for the little ones to help with and a very good substitute for the brand name version that's advertised with the clown who has very big feet.

The Grandfather

Ingredients

100g milk or dark chocolate, broken into chunks
Squirty cream
100g cornflakes
Finely chopped Strawberries

Method

Fill a saucepan with water, and boil.
Place an heat resistant bowl over the boiling water and let the chocolate melt.

Put the cornflakes in a food bag and crush using a rolling pin.

Once the chocolate has melted, remove the bowl carefully from over the saucepan and add the cornflakes.

Spread onto a greaseproof lined baking tray and let it cool right down.

Transfer to the fridge for a couple of hours.

Add the cornflake mixture into a food bag and crush with a rolling pin. Then add the chopped-up strawberries.

Now to assemble....in a bowl or glass add a squirt of cream, then some cornflake crumble, continue until you fill the bowl and top with some more of your cornflake crumble and a strawberry.

Paul James

CHINESE CHOPPED CHICKEN CURRY WITH RICE

Once again back to my childhood memories and it's something I love to reminisce with the Grandchildren as I did with my own children.

My mom and I use to go and visit my Nan up in the centre of Birmingham, I always remember it was Thursday nights as my Aunties had their own particular nights visiting Nan.

Looking out from the window of Nan's flat in the tower block where she lived was mesmerising, I could see the whole of Birmingham lighting up in the dark of the night, my mom, who was petrified of heights herself, panicking that I was to close to the window, which was of the push out type(no safety catches as I can recall, because you could spin the windows round to clean them) I'm sure this is where I got my own fear of heights from. My own Mom's anxiety of heights herself.

Sometimes one or two of my other aunts and cousins may have popped in, which for a little lad of my age was great because I knew I would get a bit more "pocket money" 50p here £1 there, it all adds up. And I knew where I would be spending it…The Chinese takeaway.

The journey home at 9 o'clock at night on the bus was always interesting, all types of people shouting, swearing and laughing, not that I was taking much notice…I was thinking of my Chopped Chicken Curry I was going to buy and also to busy staring down at the bus drivers bald head that you could do in them days, as he would look up through a small window above his head to see what was going on upstairs.

Plus I was to occupied pretending to drive the bus using the handles at the front as a steering wheel.

Now at this stage telling my story to the Grandchildren…one thing troubled them….who was holding my iPad!!!

Anyway this is my take on a beautiful memory.

Ingredients

2 Chicken breasts chopped
1 large onion finely sliced.

Cup of cooked peas
Half a cup of raisins or sultanas.
1 tbsp of vegetable oil.
Cooked Rice
Jar of your Chinese curry sauce

Method

Heat the oven to 180c.
Wrap the onion, skin and all, no oil, in a sheet of foil.
Place onto a baking tray and cook for about 30-45 minutes or until the onion is soft.

Remove from the oven and let it completely cool down. Once it's cooled down remove the foil, cut the onion in half and push the soft flesh out onto a chopping board and slice.

Heat some vegetable oil in a hot frying pan or wok.

Add the chicken, resist trying to stir at this stage as the chicken will only stick and break up.
Once the chicken is nice and brown, add the sliced-up onion.

Cook further until the onions start going slightly golden but not burnt.

Add the peas, Curry sauce and simmer until the chicken is thoroughly cooked throughout.
Serve with some rice.

Freddie and grandad

MARINATED GINGER & LIME MELON KEBABS

A little bit of fun here for the little ones (make sure you have some plasters ready!! Only joking but just be careful of the sharp points of the skewers. Which ADULTS after skewering can cut the ends off with scissors)

This is a very simple melon dessert that will activate your child's mind and taste buds.

Tingling hot, sour and delightfully sweet.

Ingredients

Melon cut into cubes
Small piece of peeled grated Ginger about an inch in size.

2 tbsps of muscavado sugar
1 tbsps of lime zest
Juice of 1 lime
Scatter of coriander

Method

In a large tightly sealed container add all of the ingredients
and place in the fridge for at least a couple of hours.

Under adult supervision skewer the melon cubes onto the
sticks, scatter with coriander and watch how little ones
minds and taste buds react to the contrasting flavours.

KIDS POSH HAM & CHEESE TOASTIE OR CROQUE MADAME

I think everyone a some stage had a sandwich maker, its probably now been pushed to the back of the cupboard along with the boiled egg topper, taco holder and pizza scissors....like mine.

Kids love something different and sometimes not letting them know all of the ingredients by name such as Gruyere Cheese...just cheese will do and stop the "I hate that cheese, we had it at school" conversations....I mean Gruyere Cheese in school!! Come on.

I've made this before and was told it was just a posh cheese & ham toastie....AND THAT WAS BY ADULTS!!

Trust me let the kids decide, my little ones did and totally enjoyed it.

Ingredients

4 slices sourdough or crusty bread
75 grams butter
75 grams grated cheddar cheese
75 grams grated gruyere cheese
4 thick slices of good quality ham
125 ml milk
2 bay leaves

1 small onion chopped in quarters
20 grams plain flour
2 tbsp heaped Dijon mustard
Good splash of Worcestershire sauce

Method

Make a simple béchamel sauce. Using milk, bay leaves and a small onion. Add the Dijon mustard, a little Worcestershire sauce and the cheddar cheese. It should be a thick creamy sauce with a dark deep flavour (well that's how I like it but by all means use less of the mustard). Season to taste all the time.

Then with your slices of sourdough bread spread a little butter on one side and grill until golden (one side only) Turn the bread over and spread each slice with a thin layer of the béchamel sauce and add generous slices of ham.

Add your grated gruyère cheese and form into a sandwich.

In a frying pan melt some butter and fry gently on both sides until golden.

Transfer to a preheated oven and cook for 4-5 minutes so it warms right through to the centre.

Now fry an egg and plate up with a bit of salad.

CORNISH SPLITS

Cornwall without a doubt is my spiritual home, Cornwall has always been in my heart – magical and mystical, rugged coastlines with waves crashing against the rocks and beautiful beaches with golden sands.

Lovely childhood memories of running across the dunes at Perran Sands, playing football on the beach with my family, then as I got older, watching my own children and then grandchildren experience the same wonderful memories and loving family holidays as I did.

This recipe is one I've taken from numerous versions I've found in books etc, but with a little twist….

The twist being the plating up and construction of the dish by my adorable Grandchildren.

Ingredients

250g of strong white flour
50g of plain flour
45g of butter
Half of a small packet of yeast (around 15g)
1 tsp of sugar
A pinch of salt
125ml of milk

Method

The method is very similar to the way you make bread. First, put the flour and salt into a bowl and rub in the butter.

Next feed the yeast with a little luke-warm water and all of the sugar. Leave it for a couple of minutes to activate and then mix it with the warm milk.

Pour the milk into the flour mixture a little at a time and bring it all together into a dough.

Once you have the dough you need to leave it to prove. Cover it with a tea towel and leave it somewhere dry and warm, like an airing cupboard.

After 20 minutes, the dough should have doubled in size. Take it out and knead it for a few minutes, before splitting into your splits.

Then leave them to prove once more, so that they double in size again.

At that point you can place them on grease proof paper on a baking tray and then cook at 180C for around 18 to 20 minutes, or until golden brown.

After you take them out of the oven, leave them to cool a little, but while they are still warm split them apart and cover them in jam and clotted cream – perfect.

GREAT NANS BEST STEW EVER

I wrote a recipe in an article once called "My Mom's Stew" If Cooking is all about memories this dish to me and my family is top of the list.

Now I wanted to, not adapt or change the recipe but to explain to my little ones the family closeness of days in the past through to nowadays.

This is why I'm changing the name to "Great Nan's Stew" unfortunately she passed away before any of my grandchildren were born, in fact my youngest son, Jay was born just couple of months after my mom passed away, so he never had the chance to feel the love and warmth of his Nan.

But her photo is always on show just like my dad's, grandad, and great grandad to the kids. They will never forget who they are.

Fortunately, I passed on this family unit of togetherness to my own children, which they have passed on to their children, "My Beautiful Grandchildren"

I remember so well as a little lad smelling the comforting warmth of the stew wafting around the kitchen. A big saucepan of comforting stew that lasted a few days, always being topped up with potatoes and peas each day to make it last.

A well-known saying that my mom always used to say " it always tastes better the next day " is something that my own children say as I serve up this dish with Dumplings and crusty bread.

Ingredients

400 g lean beef mince
400 g stewing beef
Selection of carrots, turnips, swede
1 litre vegetable stock
Salt & pepper
Gravy Granules with two oxo cubes.
1 tbsp olive oil

Method

Roughly chop the vegetables and gently fry with a little olive oil to colour and seal in the flavour. In a separate pan dry fry the beef mince and stewing beef until the beef is slightly caramelised. Add the vegetable stock to the vegetables and bring to the boil. Add a sprinkle of gravy granules to the meat mix and stir.

Combine the meat with the vegetables and stir till it comes to boil. Lower the heat and cook slowly for "hours" pinching a bowl of this comforting dish whenever you want.

Next day top up with more potatoes and peas, gravy and keep enjoying.

I usually make my lovely version of a "Cornish pasty" out of the last of the stew.

Summer-Rai and granddad

ROASTED LAMB FROM GREECE

I have met some amazing people in the last couple of years from Greece, mainly Corfu. I've never come across so many people that are so giving, caring and hospitable.

With a few projects in the pipeline, I'm hoping one day I will be taking my Grandchildren to visit these beautiful islands and country.

I can just imagine them sitting by the side of the harbour in my favourite place of Kassiopi taking in the amazing views and scenery and sampling the local delicacies it offers, while the smell of Greek Coffee wafts through the air.

Bliss!!

Ingredients

2 lamb shanks
1 bulb garlic (2 cloves thinly sliced)
2 lemons (halved) retain some zest
1 tbs dried oregano
8 new potatoes
4 bay leaves
200ml white wine
Greek sea Salt flakes
black pepper
1 red onion cut into chunks
olive oil
A couple of sprigs of Rosemary

Method

Place the lamb shanks into a deep cooking tray.

With a sharp knife, make small incisions about 5-10mm deep around the lamb.

Crush open a bulb of garlic, keeping 2 cloves to thinly slice into slithers.

Insert the **garlic slithers** into the lamb and scatter the rest of the garlic around the tray.

Add all the rest of the ingredients to the tray including the juice of the lemons.

Tightly seal the tray with a couple of layers of foil and refrigerate overnight (or at least a couple of hours)

Remove the tray from the fridge and let it come to room temperature.

In the meantime pre-heat the oven to 180°C

Place the tray, still sealed with the foil into the oven and reduce the temperature to 140°C and cook slowly for three hours.

Remove from the oven, discard foil, squeeze the lemon and spoon the juices over your lamb and return back to the oven for a further one hour at 180°C

Remove from the oven, let the lamb rest for a good half hour then serve with your lovely steam baked lemon and garlic infused potatoes.

MINCE BEEF PIE

A perfect dish to get the little ones involved with, rolling the pastry, filling the pie and eggy washing the pastry, not forgetting to let them decorate the top with pastry leaves.

Memories of my childhood were very special, loving parents and two sisters and one brother who were and still are very close....I'm lucky.

Also a huge and influential part of my childhood was a lovely couple and their family who lived next door to ours.

Auntie Win who I mentioned earlier looked after me while my Mom and Dad was at work, was the one person who was my inspiration for my love for homemade cooking, Proper warm, comforting food that always brought me running into her kitchen from playing outside in the Garden.

Always fish on a Friday, Sausage and Mash maybe on a Wednesday, where I was allowed to help mash the potatoes with the same potato masher I still use to today.

But always my favourite which was usually on Tuesday's was Aunty Win's homemade pie with peas and boiled potatoes, with Bisto gravy. A small round plate lay in the middle of the small kitchen table with "ROUNDS OF BREAD AND BUTTER, CUT IN HALF"placed on it and the three of us, Auntie Win, my Uncle Alf and myself would sit down to eat at about midday.

This Pie that I cooked is in memory of "My Auntie Win" and them Tuesday Pie and potato days over 40 years ago.

Ingredients

1onion finely chopped
500g beef mince
1 cup water
2 beef stock cubes
1/4 cup tomato sauce (not purée)
2 tsp Worcestershire sauce
1 pinch salt and pepper to taste
3 tbs of corn starch or thickening agent.
2 sheets of ready-made shortcrust pastry
1 egg to glaze

Method

Cook meat and onion until meat is well browned.
Add ¾ cup water, stock cubes, sauces and seasonings.
Bring to the boil and simmer for 15 minutes. Blend corn starch and the remaining water, add to meat, bring to the boil and simmer for 5 minutes. Cool right down.

Then slightly grease with butter, a pie dish and line your rolled out shortcrust pastry and 'blind bake' (pre-baking a crust can ensure that your pie crust will be fully baked and browned and not soggy) for 10 minutes.

Remove from the oven and spoon in the cooled meat mixture. Slightly moisten the edges of pastry with water.

Top with the other rolled out shortcrust pastry, pressing down to seal the edges, trim and glaze with egg.
Bake at 180c for 25-30 minutes until golden.

Freya and granddad

BV - #0076 - 061221 - C73 - 210/148/5 - PB - 9781913839369 - Gloss Lamination